Table of Contents

T0243128

General Information

Projects

It's Owl Good Blanket, *page 10*

Clever Fox Blanket, *page 18*

Meet the Designer

Christine Naugle is the designer and owner of Sweet Potato 3 crochet patterns. She finds inspiration for her designs through the beauty, textures and colors she sees in nature. Christine's goal when she designs is to create innovative patterns that teach new techniques and skills, allowing crafters to improve and be confident in their finished projects. She loves the creative process of designing and is dedicated to providing detailed, high-quality patterns. Christine feels blessed to have the opportunity to design crochet patterns for all of you. Her greatest reward is seeing the beautiful works made from her designs, so make sure to share yours with her by tagging @sweetpotato3patterns on Facebook or Instagram.

When Christine is not crocheting you can find her spending time with family doing "all things outdoors." A mother of three active kids and married to an adventurous husband, she can often be found on a whitewater rafting adventure, paddling on a SUP, snow skiing, camping, hiking, biking, or enjoying a nice cup of coffee or glass of wine on her back deck overlooking the mountains in Idaho.

Scan QR code for the designer's course to learn everything you need to know about crocheting this style of blanket.

Need help?
Stitch Guide.com
ILLUSTRATED GUIDES
HOW-TO VIDEOS

Special Stitches to Get You Started

Each of the woodland blankets in this book uses special stitches to make the design really stand out. This section includes the illustrations, photos and instructions to learn the stitches. As you work the blanket patterns, be sure to refer to these illustrations and photos for those stitches. Once you've mastered the stitches, you'll be on your way to creating all these beautiful blankets!

Stitch Tutorial

Special Stitches

First foundation half double crochet (first foundation hdc): Ch 2, yo, insert hook in 2nd ch from hook *(see illustration A)*, yo, pull up a lp, yo, draw through 1 lp on hook *(see illustration B—ch-1 completed)*, yo, draw through all lps on hook *(see illustrations C and D—hdc completed)*.

Next foundation half double crochet (next foundation hdc): *Yo, insert hook in last ch-1 made *(see illustration A)*, yo, pull up a lp, yo, draw through 1 lp on hook *(see illustration B—ch-1 completed)*, yo, draw through all lps on hook *(see illustrations C and D—hdc completed)*, rep from * as indicated.

Beginning knotted half double crochet (beg khdc): Ch 1, yo, insert hook in ch-1 sp;

pull up a lp *(3 lps on hook)*;

yo, insert hook in next st, pull up a lp *(5 lps on hook)*;

yo, pull through all 5 lps on hook—khdc has been completed.

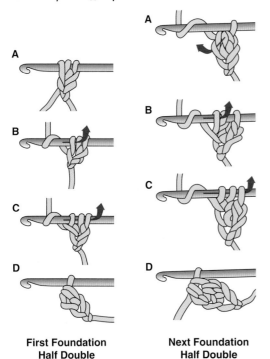

First Foundation Half Double Crochet Stitch

Next Foundation Half Double Crochet Stitch

Next knotted half double crochet (next khdc):

Beg next khdc in same sp as last khdc ended in;

yo, insert hook in same st as last st completed and pull up a lp, yo, insert hook in next st and pull up a lp *(5 lps on hook)*;

yo, pull through all 5 lps on hook.

Rep these steps across row.

Last knotted half double crochet (last khdc):

Yo, insert hook in same st the last khdc ended in;

pull up a lp, yo, insert hook in beg ch of last row;

pull up a lp *(5 lps on hook)*;

yo, pull through all 5 lps to complete khdc.

Note: *Notice this st is aligned right on top of the first st of the prior row.*

Special Techniques

Foundation Half Double Crochet Color Change

Work foundation row until 1 st before the color change is indicated. Work the st until the last pull-through, 3 lps will be left on hook.

Using new color, pull a lp through all 3 lps on hook to complete the st.

Complete the next foundation hdc in the new color.

Color Change Instructions

When changing colors, drop the prior color to the back of the project; when turning at the end of the row, the dropped yarn will be on the working side.

To keep yarn from twisting while working, alternate the direction of your rotation (turn) at the end of each row. (Turn clockwise on even rows and counterclockwise on odd rows.)

If using the technique of carrying the unused main color behind the contrasting color sts, be sure to pull the unused main color yarn a little taut when picking it back up again to use. Don't pull it too tight though as you don't want it to create a pucker.

Check the stitch count at the end of each row.

Complete prior st until last yo *(5 lps on hook)*.

Using new color, yo and pull through all 5 lps on hook.

Continue next khdc with new color, beg the next st in the same st as the last st completed.

Complete the st in the new yarn color.

Changing yarn colors before the aligned color change:

If color change is before the change in the previous row, complete the last st before the color change until the last yo.

Using the new color, yo and pull through all lps to complete the khdc. Make sure this is loose enough that you can crochet over it in the next sts.

Continue to work the khdc over the new color while working the next sts; after the sts are crocheted, the yarn is buried leaving a clean color change.

Changing yarn colors after the aligned color change:

If color change is after the change in the previous row, pull up the color change yarn where it changed in the prior row.

Work the khdc over the yarn color burying it under the st.

Continue to bury the yarn under sts until you reach the next color change.

Change yarn in the last pull-through of the prior st.

Then, continue with the new color in the next st. ●

Forest Pine Blanket

Bring nature and charm into your living space
with this unique design.

Skill Level

 **INTERMEDIATE**

Finished Measurements

40 inches wide x 52 inches long

Materials

- Premier Spun Colors medium (worsted) weight acrylic/fine merino superwash yarn (7 oz/ 419 yds/200g per cake):
    - 3 cakes #1110-12 rustic (MC)
- Premier Anti-Pilling Everyday Worsted medium (worsted) weight acrylic yarn (3½ oz/180 yds/100g per skein):
    - 6 skeins #100-68 Aran (CC)
- Size I/9/5.5mm crochet hook or size needed to obtain gauge
- Size K/10½/6.5mm crochet hook
- Tapestry needle
- Bobbins (optional)

Gauge

With I hook: 12 khdc = 4 inches; 10 rows = 4 inches

Pattern Notes

The beginning of this blanket has color changes in the foundation row. Use bobbins for working this row just like the rest of the blanket.

Crochet the foundation row loosely so it will allow for the same ease/tension as the rest of the blanket.

After the foundation row has been completed, the remainder of the blanket is worked using the smaller hook.

Count stitches at the end of each row to ensure that you have the correct stitch count. The last stitch can easily be overlooked or skipped.

Make sure you follow the correct color changes for each row.

Each row will have a total of 120 knotted half double crochet stitches. There is a total of 130 rows.

Each square on the Chart represents 1 knotted half double crochet.

Chain-1 at the beginning of each row is not counted as a stitch.

When changing yarn colors, always drop the color of yarn not in use to the back of your work. As you work the next row, the yarn will be on the working side.

This blanket has no border.

Weave in ends as work progresses.

At the end of each row alternate turning clockwise and counterclockwise. This will keep your yarn from tangling.

Blanket

Row 1 (RS): With larger hook and MC, work **first foundation hdc** (see Stitch Tutorial on page 2), work 59 **next foundation hdc** (see Stitch Tutorial), **change to CC** (see Pattern Notes and Stitch Tutorial), work 60 next foundation half double crochet, turn. (120 hdc)

Row 2: With smaller hook, **ch 1** (See Pattern Notes), work **beg khdc** (see Stitch Tutorial), work 59 **next khdc** (see Stitch Tutorial), change to MC, work 59 next khdc, work **last khdc** (see Stitch Tutorial), turn. (120 khdc)

Row 3: Ch 1, work beg khdc, work 59 next khdc, change to CC, work 59 next khdc, work last khdc, turn.

Rows 4–17: Rep rows 2 and 3.

Row 18: Ch 1, following **Chart** (see Pattern Notes and Chart) work beg khdc, work 55 next khdc, change to MC, work 4 next khdc, change to CC, work 4 next khdc, change to MC, work 55 next khdc, work last khdc, turn.

Rows 19–130: Work as established, following Chart for color changes.

Fasten off. ●

KEY
■ MC
□ CC

Be sure to check out the designer's class to assist you with working these projects.

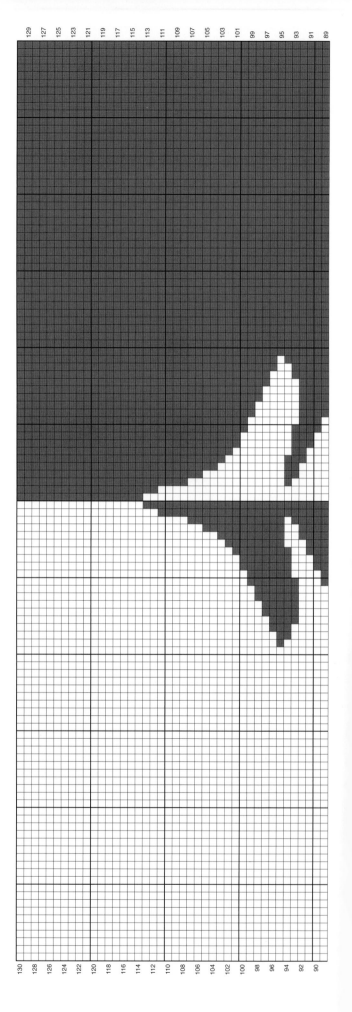

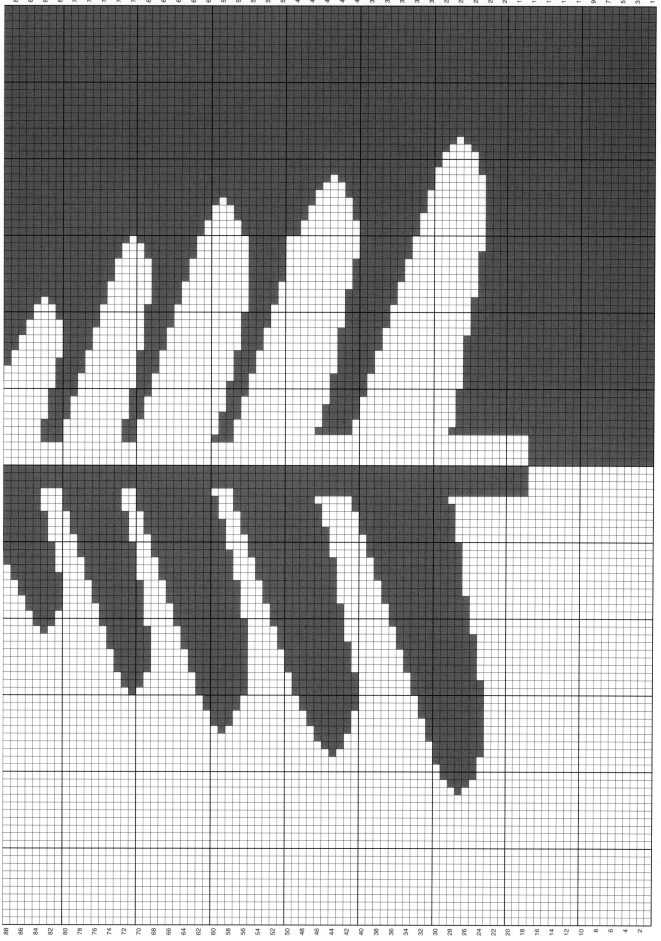

Forest Pine Blanket
Chart

It's Owl Good Blanket

This quirky owl decor will liven up any room.

Skill Level

 INTERMEDIATE

Finished Measurements

40 inches wide x 52 inches long

Materials

- Premier Spun Colors medium (worsted) weight acrylic/fine merino superwash yarn (7 oz/ 419 yds/200g per cake):
  3 cakes #1110-05 mallard (MC)
- Premier Anti-Pilling Everyday Worsted medium (worsted) weight acrylic yarn (3½ oz/180 yds/100g per skein):
  6 skeins #100-68 Aran (CC)
- Size I/9/5.5mm crochet hook or size needed to obtain gauge
- Size K/10½/6.5mm crochet hook
- Tapestry needle
- Bobbins (optional)

Gauge

With I hook: 12 khdc = 4 inches; 10 rows = 4 inches

Pattern Notes

The beginning of this blanket has color changes in the foundation row. Use bobbins for working this row just like the rest of the blanket.

Crochet the foundation row loosely so it will allow for the same ease/tension as the rest of the blanket.

After the foundation row has been completed, the remainder of the blanket is worked using the smaller hook.

Count stitches at the end of each row to ensure that you have the correct stitch count. The last stitch can easily be overlooked or skipped.

Make sure you follow the correct color changes for each row.

Each row will have a total of 120 knotted half double crochet stitches. There is a total of 130 rows.

Each square on the Chart represents 1 knotted half double crochet.

Chain-1 at the beginning of each row is not counted as a stitch.

When changing yarn colors, always drop the color of yarn not in use to the back of your work. As you work the next row, the yarn will be on the working side.

This blanket has no border.

Weave in ends as work progresses.

At the end of each row alternate turning clockwise and counterclockwise. This will keep your yarn from tangling.

Blanket

Row 1 (RS): With larger hook and CC, work **first foundation hdc** *(see Stitch Tutorial on page 2)*, work 59 **next foundation hdc** *(see Stitch Tutorial)*, **change to MC** *(see Pattern Notes and Stitch Tutorial)*, work 60 next foundation half double crochet, turn. *(120 hdc)*

Row 2: With smaller hook, **ch 1** *(see Pattern Notes)*, work **beg khdc** *(see Stitch Tutorial)*, work 59 **next khdc** *(see Stitch Tutorial)*, change to CC, work 59 next khdc, work **last khdc** *(see Stitch Tutorial)*, turn. *(120 khdc)*

Row 3: Ch 1, work beg khdc, work 59 next khdc, change to MC, work 59 next khdc, work last khdc, turn.

Rows 4–19: Rep rows 2 and 3.

Row 20: Ch 1, following **Chart** *(see Pattern Notes and Chart)* work beg khdc, work 58 next khdc, change to CC, work 1 next khdc, change to MC, work 1 next khdc, change to CC, work 58 next khdc, work last khdc, turn.

Rows 21–130: Work as established, following Chart for color changes.

Fasten off.

KEY	
■	MC
□	CC

Try different variegated yarns paired with solids for looks to match everyone's style.

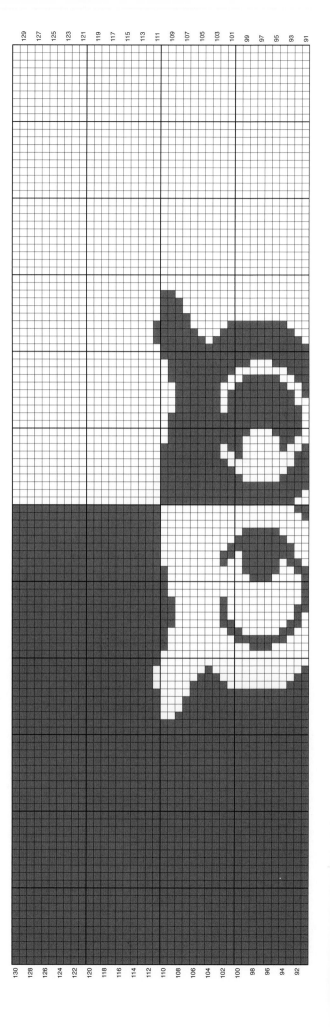

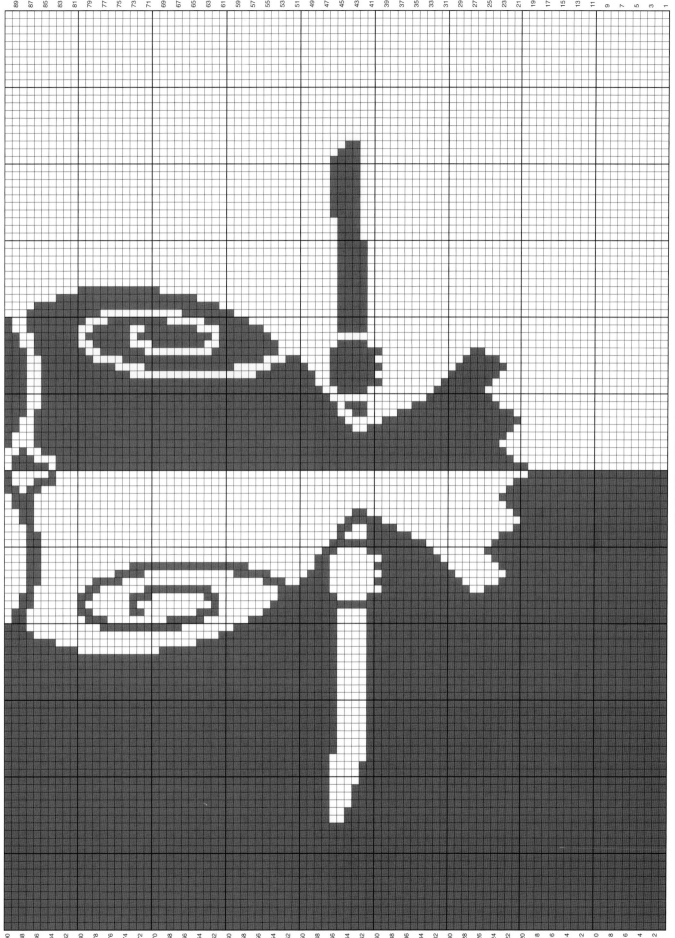

It's Owl Good Blanket
Chart

Camp Fireside Blanket

Make this fun blanket for your camping buddies so they can bring the ambience of the outdoors into their homes.

Skill Level

 INTERMEDIATE

Finished Measurements

40 inches wide x 52 inches long

Materials

- Premier Spun Colors medium (worsted) weight acrylic/fine merino superwash yarn (7 oz/ 419 yds/200g per cake):
  3 cakes #1110-09 woodland (MC)
- Premier Anti-Pilling Everyday Worsted medium (worsted) weight acrylic yarn (3½ oz/180 yds/100g per skein):
  6 skeins #100-68 Aran (CC)
- Size I/9/5.5mm crochet hook or size needed to obtain gauge
- Size K/10½/6.5mm crochet hook
- Tapestry needle
- Bobbins (optional)

Gauge

With I hook: 12 khdc = 4 inches; 10 rows = 4 inches

Pattern Notes

The beginning of this blanket has color changes in the foundation row. Use bobbins for working this row just like the rest of the blanket.

Crochet the foundation row loosely so it will allow for the same ease/tension as the rest of the blanket.

After the foundation row has been completed, the remainder of the blanket is worked using the smaller hook.

Count stitches at the end of each row to ensure that you have the correct stitch count. The last stitch can easily be overlooked or skipped.

Make sure you follow the correct color changes for each row.

Each row will have a total of 120 knotted half double crochet stitches. There is a total of 130 rows.

Each square on the Chart represents 1 knotted half double crochet.

Chain-1 at the beginning of each row is not counted as a stitch.

When changing yarn colors, always drop the color of yarn not in use to the back of your work. As you work the next row, the yarn will be on the working side.

This blanket has no border.

Weave in ends as work progresses.

At the end of each row alternate turning clockwise and counterclockwise. This will keep your yarn from tangling.

Blanket

Row 1 (RS): With larger hook and MC, work **first foundation hdc** (see Stitch Tutorial on page 2), work 59 **next foundation hdc** (see Stitch Tutorial), **change to CC** (see Pattern Notes and Stitch Tutorial), work 60 next foundation half double crochet, turn. (120 hdc)

Row 2: With smaller hook, **ch 1** (See Pattern Notes), work **beg khdc** (see Stitch Tutorial), work 59 **next khdc** (see Stitch Tutorial), change to MC, work 59 next khdc, work **last khdc** (see Stitch Tutorial), turn. (120 khdc)

Row 3: Ch 1, work beg khdc, work 59 next khdc, change to CC, work 59 next khdc, work last khdc, turn.

Rows 4–11: Rep rows 2 and 3.

Row 12: Rep row 2.

Row 13: Ch 1, following **Chart** (see Pattern Notes and Chart) work beg khdc, work 43 next khdc, change to CC, work 4 next khdc, change to MC, work 12 next khdc, change to CC, work 13 next khdc, change to MC, work 5 next khdc, change to CC, work 41 khdc, work last khdc, turn.

Rows 14–130: Work as established, following Chart for color changes.

Fasten off. ●

KEY	
■	MC
□	CC

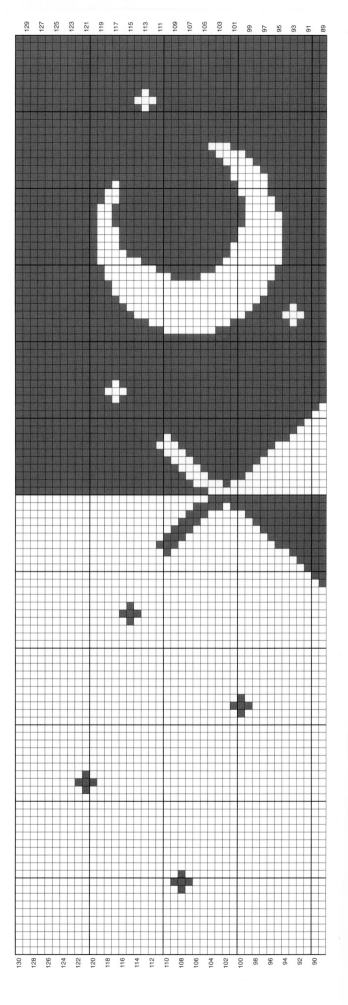

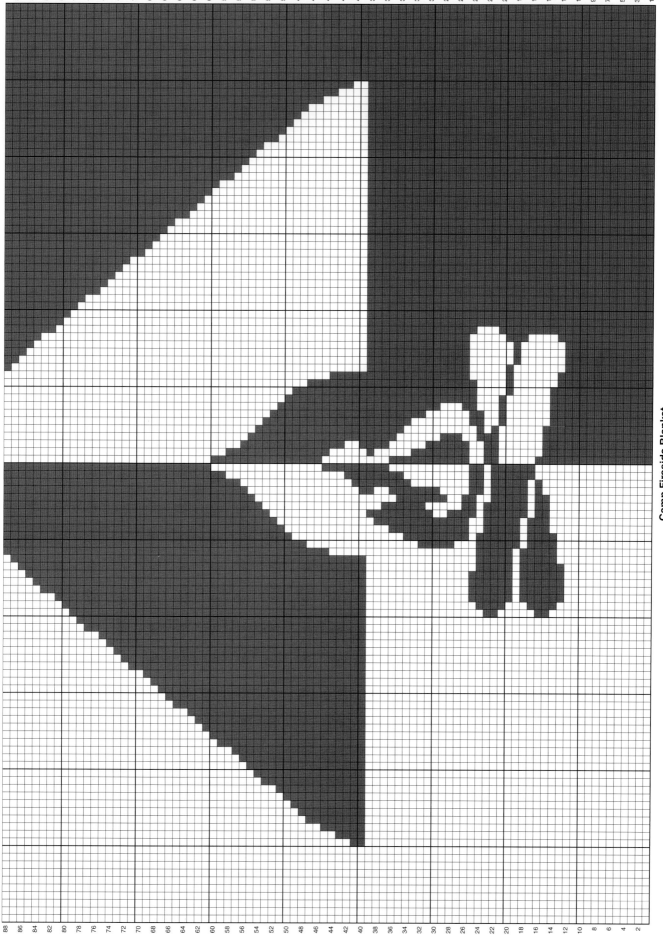

Camp Fireside Blanket
Chart

Clever Fox Blanket

You will want to whip up several versions of this adorable fox and give one to each person in your family.

Skill Level

 INTERMEDIATE

Finished Measurements

40 inches wide x 52 inches long

Materials

- Premier Spun Colors medium (worsted) weight acrylic/fine merino superwash yarn (7 oz/ 419 yds/200g per cake):
  3 cakes #1110-11 autumn (MC)
- Premier Anti-Pilling Everyday Worsted medium (worsted) weight acrylic yarn (3½ oz/180 yds/100g per skein):
  6 skeins #100-68 Aran (CC)
- Size I/9/5.5mm crochet hook or size needed to obtain gauge
- Size K/10½/6.5mm crochet hook
- Tapestry needle
- Bobbins (optional)

Gauge

With I hook: 12 khdc = 4 inches; 10 rows = 4 inches

Pattern Notes

The beginning of this blanket has color changes in the foundation row. Use bobbins for working this row just like the rest of the blanket.

Crochet the foundation row loosely so it will allow for the same ease/tension as the rest of the blanket.

After the foundation row has been completed, the remainder of the blanket is worked using the smaller hook.

Count stitches at the end of each row to ensure that you have the correct stitch count. The last stitch can easily be overlooked or skipped.

Make sure you follow the correct color changes for each row.

Each row will have a total of 120 knotted half double crochet stitches. There is a total of 130 rows.

Each square on the Chart represents 1 knotted half double crochet.

Chain-1 at the beginning of each row is not counted as a stitch.

When changing yarn colors, always drop the color of yarn not in use to the back of your work. As you work the next row, the yarn will be on the working side.

This blanket has no border.

Weave in ends as work progresses.

At the end of each row alternate turning clockwise and counterclockwise. This will keep your yarn from tangling.

Blanket

Row 1 (RS): With larger hook and MC, work **first foundation hdc** *(see Stitch Tutorial on page 2)*, work 59 **next foundation hdc** *(see Stitch Tutorial)*, **change to CC** *(see Pattern Notes and Stitch Tutorial)*, work 60 next foundation half double crochet, turn. *(120 hdc)*

Row 2: With smaller hook, **ch 1** *(see Pattern Notes)*, work **beg khdc** *(see Stitch Tutorial)*, work 59 **next khdc** *(see Stitch Tutorial)*, change to MC, work 59 next khdc, work **last khdc** *(see Stitch Tutorial)*, turn. *(120 khdc)*

Row 3: Ch 1, work beg khdc, work 59 next khdc, change to CC, work 59 next khdc, work last khdc, turn.

Rows 4–15: Rep rows 2 and 3.

Row 16: Ch 1, following **Chart** *(see Chart and Pattern Notes)* work beg khdc, work 41 next khdc, change to MC, work 10 next khdc, change to CC, work 9 next khdc, change to MC, work 59 next khdc, work last khdc, turn.

Rows 17–130: Work as established, following Chart for color changes.

Fasten off. ●

KEY	
■	MC
□	CC

It could be fun to play around and work up these blankets in two solid yarns.

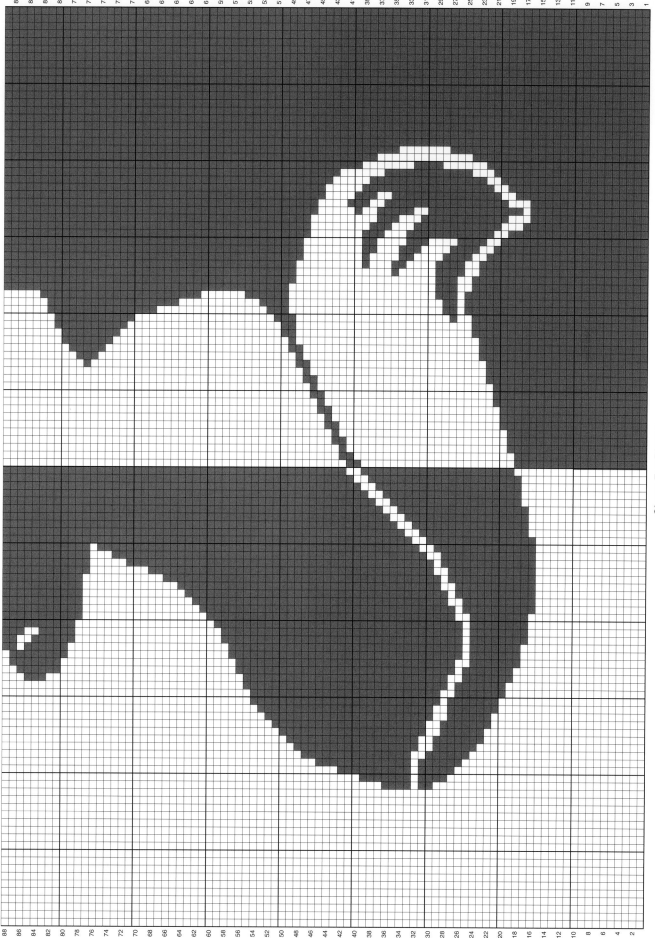

Clever Fox Blanket
Chart

Feeling Squirrelly Blanket

Put a smile on someone's face by gifting them this rascally little critter with a container of mixed nuts.

Skill Level

 INTERMEDIATE

Finished Measurements

40 inches wide x 52 inches long

Materials

- Premier Spun Colors medium (worsted) weight acrylic/fine merino superwash yarn (7 oz/ 419 yds/200g per cake):
    3 cakes #1110-14 harvest (MC)
- Premier Anti-Pilling Everyday Worsted medium (worsted) weight acrylic yarn (3½ oz/180 yds/100g per skein):
    6 skeins #100-68 Aran (CC)
- Size I/9/5.5mm crochet hook or size needed to obtain gauge
- Size K/10½/6.5mm crochet hook
- Tapestry needle
- Bobbins (optional)

Gauge

With I hook: 12 khdc = 4 inches; 10 rows = 4 inches

Pattern Notes

The beginning of this blanket has color changes in the foundation row. Use bobbins for working this row just like the rest of the blanket.

Crochet the foundation row loosely so it will allow for the same ease/tension as the rest of the blanket.

After the foundation row has been completed, the remainder of the blanket is worked using the smaller hook.

Count stitches at the end of each row to ensure that you have the correct stitch count. The last stitch can easily be overlooked or skipped.

Make sure you follow the correct color changes for each row.

Each row will have a total of 120 knotted half double crochet stitches. There is a total of 130 rows.

Each square on the Chart represents 1 knotted half double crochet.

Chain-1 at the beginning of each row is not counted as a stitch.

When changing yarn colors, always drop the color of yarn not in use to the back of your work. As you work the next row, the yarn will be on the working side.

This blanket has no border.

Weave in ends as work progresses.

At the end of each row alternate turning clockwise and counterclockwise. This will keep your yarn from tangling.

Mushroom Patch Blanket

You won't need to forage around the house to find this brightly colored mushroom design.

Skill Level

 INTERMEDIATE

Finished Measurements

40 inches wide x 52 inches long

Materials

- Premier Spun Colors medium (worsted) weight acrylic/fine merino superwash yarn (7 oz/ 419 yds/200g per cake):
    3 cakes #1110-07 canyon (MC)
- Premier Anti-Pilling Everyday Worsted medium (worsted) weight acrylic yarn (3½ oz/180 yds/100g per skein):
    6 skeins #100-68 Aran (CC)
- Size I/9/5.5mm crochet hook or size needed to obtain gauge
- Size K/10½/6.5mm crochet hook
- Tapestry needle
- Bobbins (optional)

Gauge

With I hook: 12 khdc = 4 inches; 10 rows = 4 inches

Pattern Notes

The beginning of this blanket has color changes in the foundation row. Use bobbins for working this row just like the rest of the blanket.

Crochet the foundation row loosely so it will allow for the same ease/tension as the rest of the blanket.

After the foundation row has been completed, the remainder of the blanket is worked using the smaller hook.

Count stitches at the end of each row to ensure that you have the correct stitch count. The last stitch can easily be overlooked or skipped.

Make sure you follow the correct color changes for each row.

Each row will have a total of 120 knotted half double crochet stitches. There is a total of 130 rows.

Each square on the Chart represents 1 knotted half double crochet.

Chain-1 at the beginning of each row is not counted as a stitch.

When changing yarn colors, always drop the color of yarn not in use to the back of your work. As you work the next row, the yarn will be on the working side.

This blanket has no border.

Weave in ends as work progresses.

At the end of each row alternate turning clockwise and counterclockwise. This will keep your yarn from tangling.

Blanket

Row 1 (RS): With larger hook and CC, work **first foundation hdc** (*see Stitch Tutorial on page 2*), work 59 **next foundation hdc** (*see Stitch Tutorial*), **change to MC** (*see Pattern Notes and Stitch Tutorial*), work 60 next foundation half double crochet, turn. (*120 hdc*)

Row 2: With smaller hook, **ch 1** (*See Pattern Notes*), work **beg khdc** (*see Stitch Tutorial*), work 59 **next khdc** (*see Stitch Tutorial*), change to CC, work 59 next khdc, work **last khdc** (*see Stitch Tutorial*), turn. (*120 khdc*)

Row 3: Ch 1, work beg khdc, work 59 next khdc, change to MC, work 59 next khdc, work last khdc, turn.

Rows 4–17: Rep rows 2 and 3.

Row 18: Ch 1, following **Chart** (*see Pattern Notes and Chart*) work beg khdc, work 59 next khdc, change to CC, work 6 next khdc, change to MC, work 5 next khdc, change to CC, work 48 next khdc, work last khdc, turn.

Rows 19–130: Work as established, following Chart for color changes.

Fasten off. ●

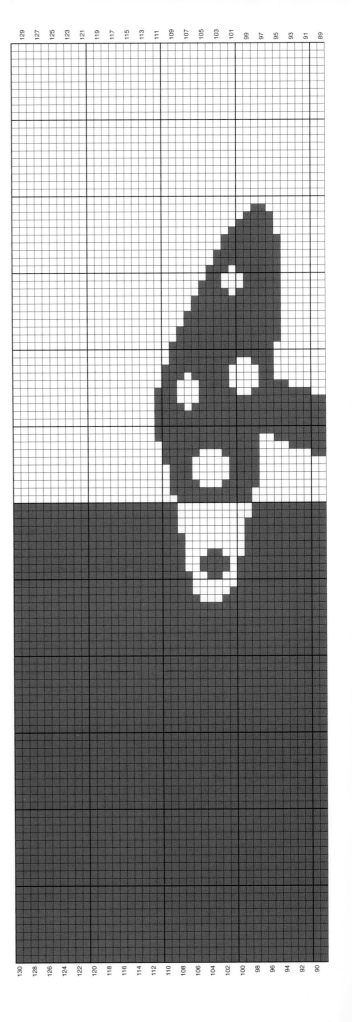

KEY	
■	MC
□	CC

Play with the silhouette in these blankets by trying a self-striping yarn with a contrasting solid for an eye-catching effect.

Mushroom Patch Blanket
Chart

STITCH GUIDE

STITCH ABBREVIATIONS

beg	begin/begins/beginning
bpdc	back post double crochet
bpsc	back post single crochet
bptr	back post treble crochet
CC	contrasting color
ch(s)	chain(s)
ch-	refers to chain or space previously made (i.e., ch-1 space)
ch sp(s)	chain space(s)
cl(s)	cluster(s)
cm	centimeter(s)
dc	double crochet (singular/plural)
dc dec	double crochet 2 or more stitches together, as indicated
dec	decrease/decreases/decreasing
dtr	double treble crochet
ext	extended
fpdc	front post double crochet
fpsc	front post single crochet
fptr	front post treble crochet
g	gram(s)
hdc	half double crochet
hdc dec	half double crochet 2 or more stitches together, as indicated
inc	increase/increases/increasing
lp(s)	loop(s)
MC	main color
mm	millimeter(s)
oz	ounce(s)
pc	popcorn(s)
rem	remain/remains/remaining
rep(s)	repeat(s)
rnd(s)	round(s)
RS	right side
sc	single crochet (singular/plural)
sc dec	single crochet 2 or more stitches together, as indicated
sk	skip/skipped/skipping
sl st(s)	slip stitch(es)
sp(s)	space(s)/spaced
st(s)	stitch(es)
tog	together
tr	treble crochet
trtr	triple treble crochet
WS	wrong side
yd(s)	yard(s)
yo	yarn over

YARN CONVERSION

OUNCES TO GRAMS		GRAMS TO OUNCES	
1	28.4	25	⅞
2	56.7	40	1⅔
3	85.0	50	1¾
4	113.4	100	3½

UNITED STATES		UNITED KINGDOM
sl st (slip stitch)	=	sc (single crochet)
sc (single crochet)	=	dc (double crochet)
hdc (half double crochet)	=	htr (half treble crochet)
dc (double crochet)	=	tr (treble crochet)
tr (treble crochet)	=	dtr (double treble crochet)
dtr (double treble crochet)	=	ttr (triple treble crochet)
skip	=	miss

Reverse single crochet (reverse sc): Ch 1, sk first st, working from left to right, insert hook in next st from front to back, draw up lp on hook, yo and draw through both lps on hook.

Chain (ch): Yo, pull through lp on hook.

Single crochet (sc): Insert hook in st, yo, pull through st, yo, pull through both lps on hook.

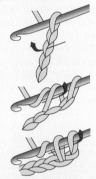

Double crochet (dc): Yo, insert hook in st, yo, pull through st, [yo, pull through 2 lps] twice.

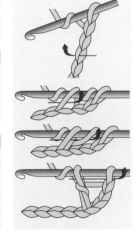

Front loop (front lp) Back loop (back lp)

Front Loop   Back Loop

Front post stitch (fp): Back post stitch (bp): When working post st, insert hook from right to left around post of st on previous row.

Back   Front

Post of Stitch

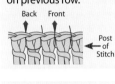

Half double crochet (hdc): Yo, insert hook in st, yo, pull through st, yo, pull through all 3 lps on hook.

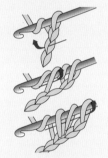

Double treble crochet (dtr): Yo 3 times, insert hook in st, yo, pull through st, [yo, pull through 2 lps] 4 times.

Slip stitch (sl st): Insert hook in st, pull through both lps on hook.

Chain color change (ch color change) Yo with new color, draw through last lp on hook.

Double crochet color change (dc color change) Drop first color, yo with new color, draw through last 2 lps of st.

Treble crochet (tr): Yo twice, insert hook in st, yo, pull through st, [yo, pull through 2 lps] 3 times.

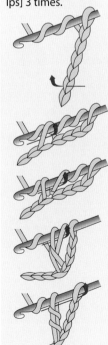

Single crochet decrease (sc dec): (Insert hook, yo, draw lp through) in each of the sts indicated, yo, draw through all lps on hook.

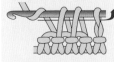

Example of 2-sc dec

Half double crochet decrease (hdc dec): (Yo, insert hook, yo, draw lp through) in each of the sts indicated, yo, draw through all lps on hook.

Example of 2-hdc dec

Double crochet decrease (dc dec): (Yo, insert hook, yo, draw lp through, yo, draw through 2 lps on hook) in each of the sts indicated, yo, draw through all lps on hook.

Example of 2-dc dec

Treble crochet decrease (tr dec): Holding back last lp of each st, tr in each of the sts indicated, yo, pull through all lps on hook.

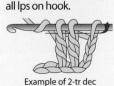

Example of 2-tr dec

Metric Conversion Charts

METRIC CONVERSIONS

yards	x	.9144	=	meters (m)
yards	x	91.44	=	centimeters (cm)
inches	x	2.54	=	centimeters (cm)
inches	x	25.40	=	millimeters (mm)
inches	x	.0254	=	meters (m)

centimeters	x	.3937	=	inches
meters	x	1.0936	=	yards

INCHES INTO MILLIMETERS & CENTIMETERS (Rounded off slightly)

inches	mm	cm	inches	cm	inches	cm	inches	cm
1/8	3	0.3	5	12.5	21	53.5	38	96.5
1/4	6	0.6	5 1/2	14	22	56	39	99
3/8	10	1	6	15	23	58.5	40	101.5
1/2	13	1.3	7	18	24	61	41	104
5/8	15	1.5	8	20.5	25	63.5	42	106.5
3/4	20	2	9	23	26	66	43	109
7/8	22	2.2	10	25.5	27	68.5	44	112
1	25	2.5	11	28	28	71	45	114.5
1 1/4	32	3.2	12	30.5	29	73.5	46	117
1 1/2	38	3.8	13	33	30	76	47	119.5
1 3/4	45	4.5	14	35.5	31	79	48	122
2	50	5	15	38	32	81.5	49	124.5
2 1/2	65	6.5	16	40.5	33	84	50	127
3	75	7.5	17	43	34	86.5		
3 1/2	90	9	18	46	35	89		
4	100	10	19	48.5	36	91.5		
4 1/2	115	11.5	20	51	37	94		

KNITTING NEEDLES CONVERSION CHART

Canada/U.S.	0	1	2	3	4	5	6	7	8	9	10	10½	11	13	15
Metric (mm)	2	2¼	2¾	3¼	3½	3¾	4	4½	5	5½	6	6½	8	9	10

CROCHET HOOKS CONVERSION CHART

Canada/U.S.	1/B	2/C	3/D	4/E	5/F	6/G	8/H	9/I	10/J	10½/K	N
Metric (mm)	2.25	2.75	3.25	3.5	3.75	4.25	5	5.5	6	6.5	9.0

Annie's® Published by Annie's, 306 East Parr Road, Berne, IN 46711. Printed in USA. Copyright © 2024 Annie's. All rights reserved. This publication may not be reproduced in part or in whole without written permission from the publisher.

RETAIL STORES: If you would like to carry this publication or any other Annie's publication, visit AnniesWSL.com.

Every effort has been made to ensure that the instructions in this publication are complete and accurate. We cannot, however, take responsibility for human error, typographical mistakes or variations in individual work. Please visit AnniesCustomerService.com to check for pattern updates.

ISBN: 979-8-89253-346-1

2 3 4 5 6 7 8 9